Tit for Tat, Jesus Is NOT about That!

JULIA SEXIL

ISBN 979-8-88851-137-4 (Paperback)
ISBN 979-8-89112-219-2 (Hardcover)
ISBN 979-8-88851-138-1 (Digital)

Copyright © 2024 Julia Sexil
All rights reserved
First Edition

All rights reserved. No part of this publication may be reproduced, distributed, or transmitted in any form or by any means, including photocopying, recording, or other electronic or mechanical methods without the prior written permission of the publisher. For permission requests, solicit the publisher via the address below.

Covenant Books
11661 Hwy 707
Murrells Inlet, SC 29576
www.covenantbooks.com

To Ariana, PJ, and Faith for whom I am
proud to be called "mommy."

To Major Marie, my big sis. Your fierce love for me has
inspired me to look up to you and call you my hero.

To Mommy Leonne and in loving memory of Papi Gercey,
thank you for teaching all nine of us kiddos the meaning
of "a family that prays together stays together."

And to my hubby and best friend for life, Mike, thank
you for always seeing the best in me especially
when I can't see it in myself. I love you.

A Special Prayer for You

Dear Heavenly Father,

I thank You so much for this very special little boy or girl today. I also thank You for creating them for a distinct purpose.

Instill in (*child's name here*) the understanding to know Your love for them will never ever be based upon what they do. Reveal to them Your love for them can never ever be earned either. Most importantly, help Your precious baby to understand Your love for them is eternally based upon *who* they are to You—*Your child*.

Carve the words *grace* and *truth* on the tablet of their heart so they will never allow their guilt and shame to keep them from running back to You.

Above all, I pray that (*child's name here*) will accept You as Father and Friend today so they can start experiencing how great You really are!

In Jesus's name, I pray.
Amen.

TIT FOR TAT—what does this mean?

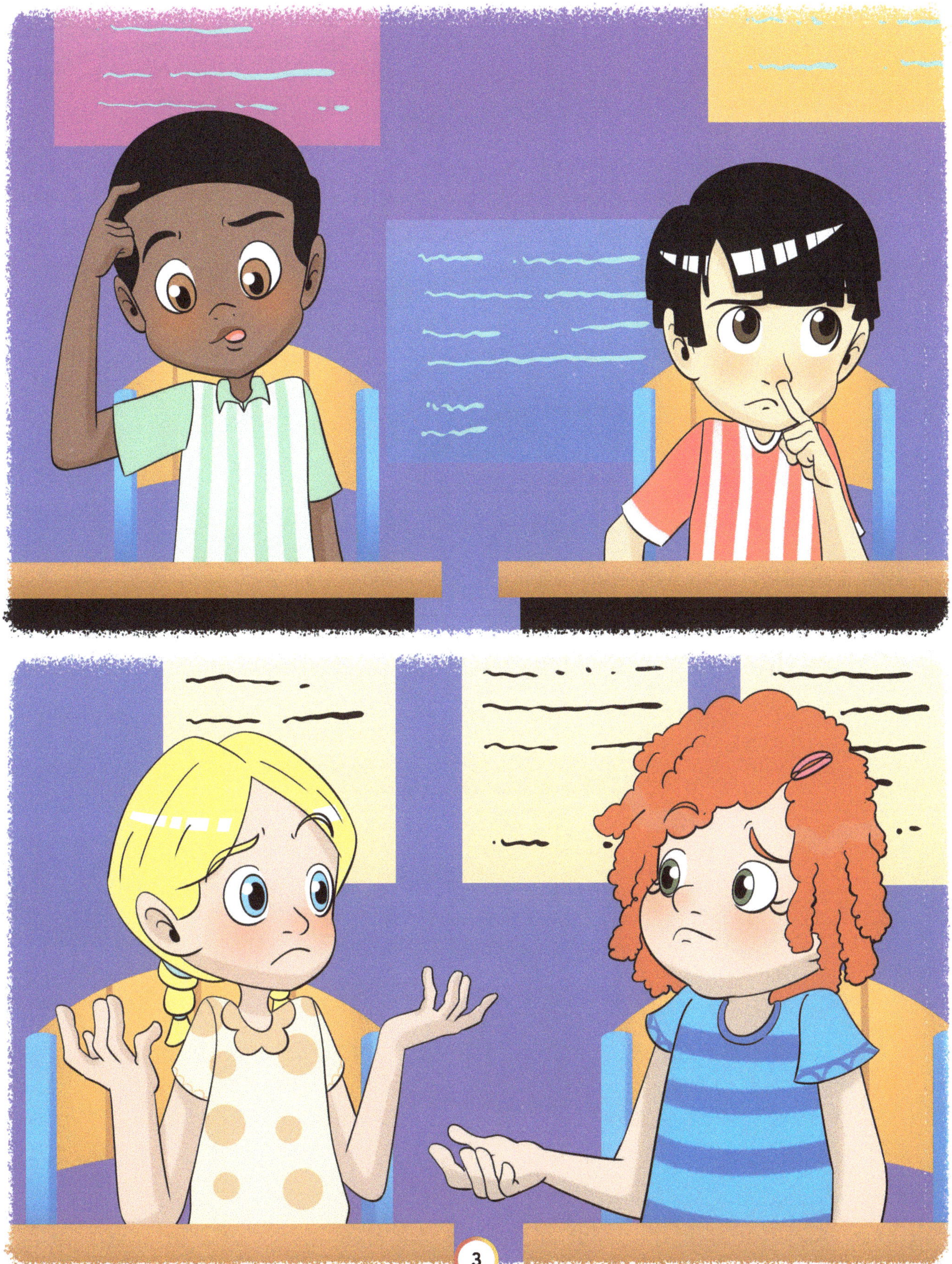

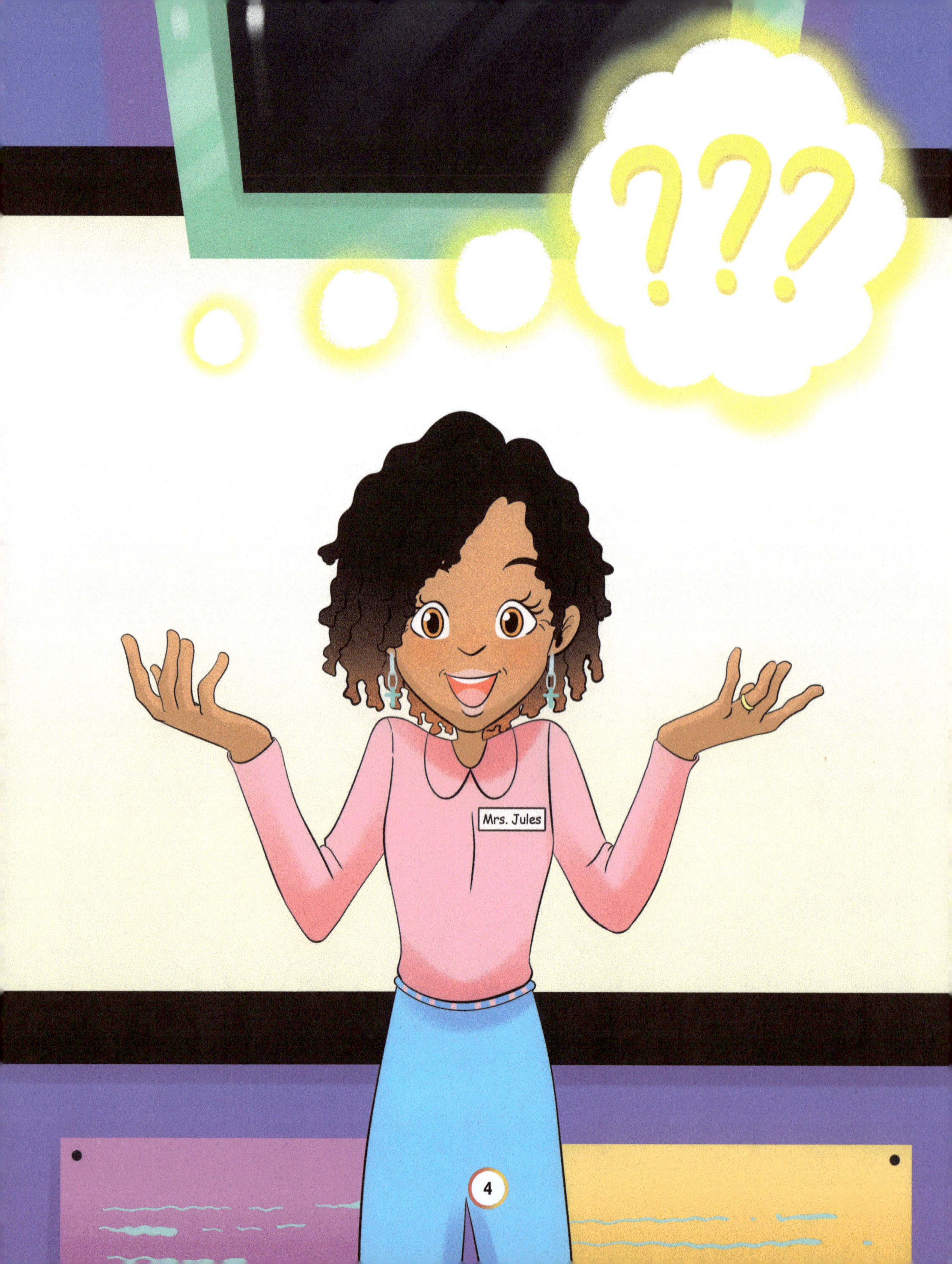
???
Mrs. Jules

Do you really want to know?

"I do to you what you've done to me."

7

This was NOT the idea Jesus wanted to show.

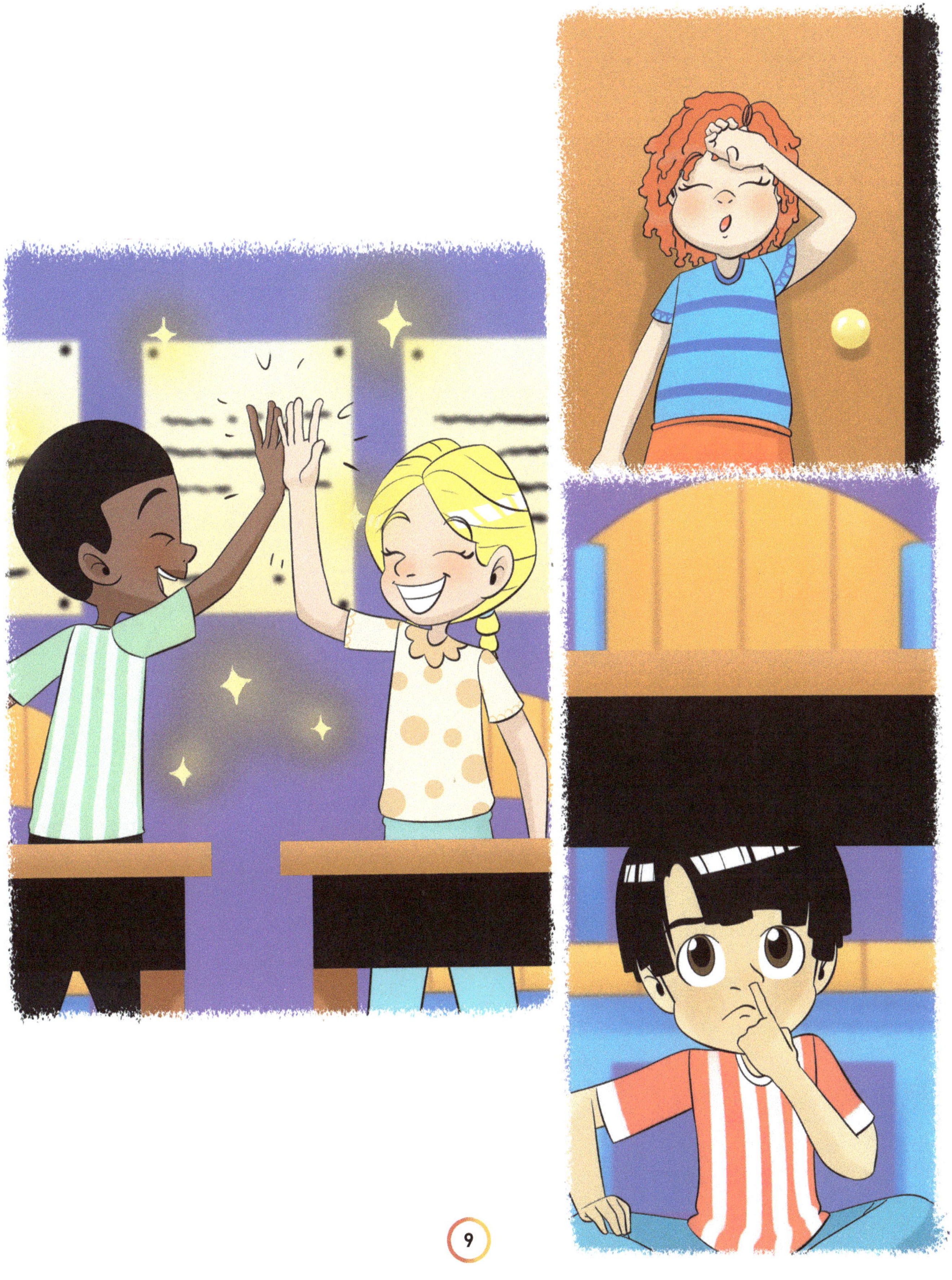

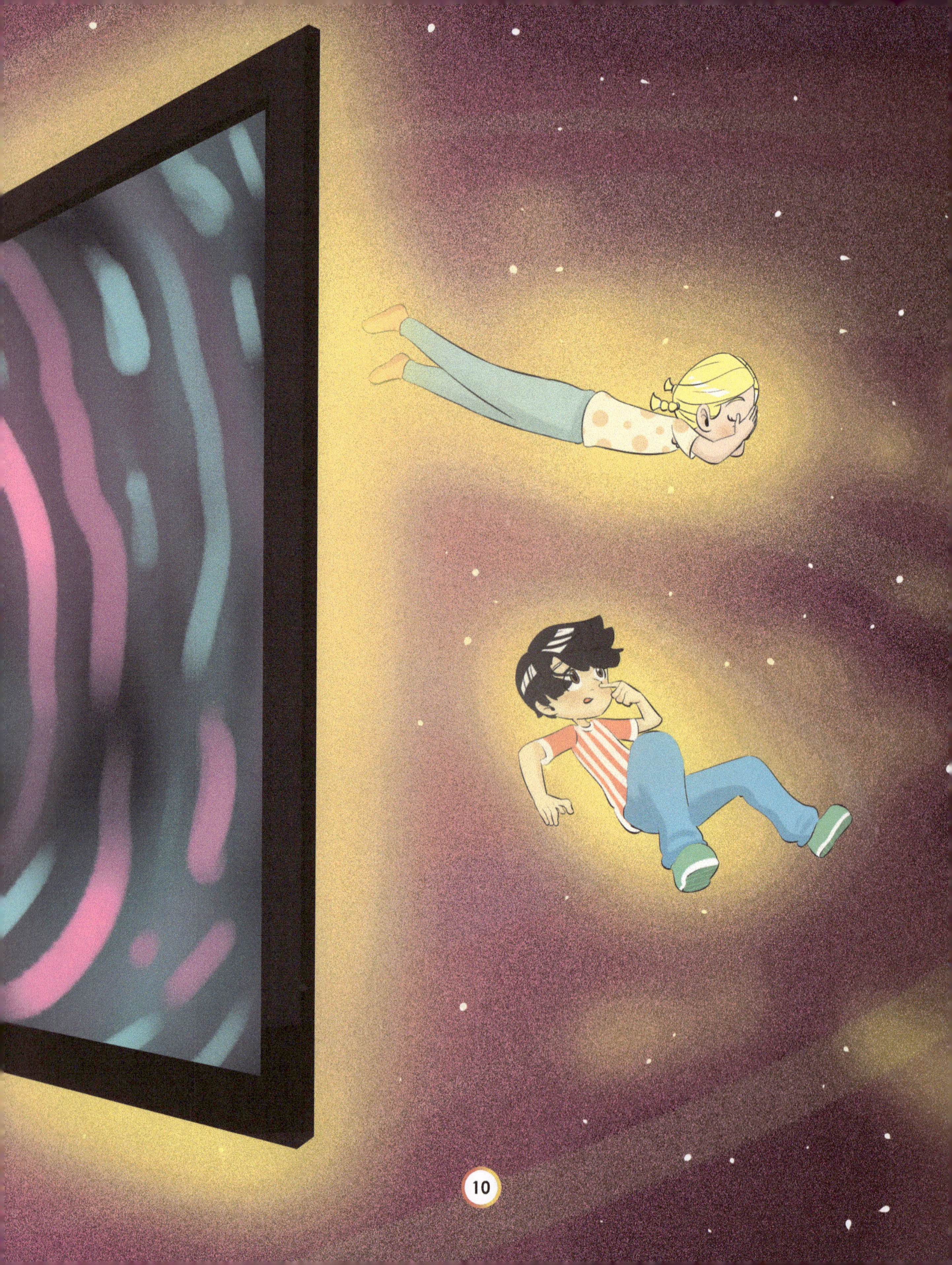

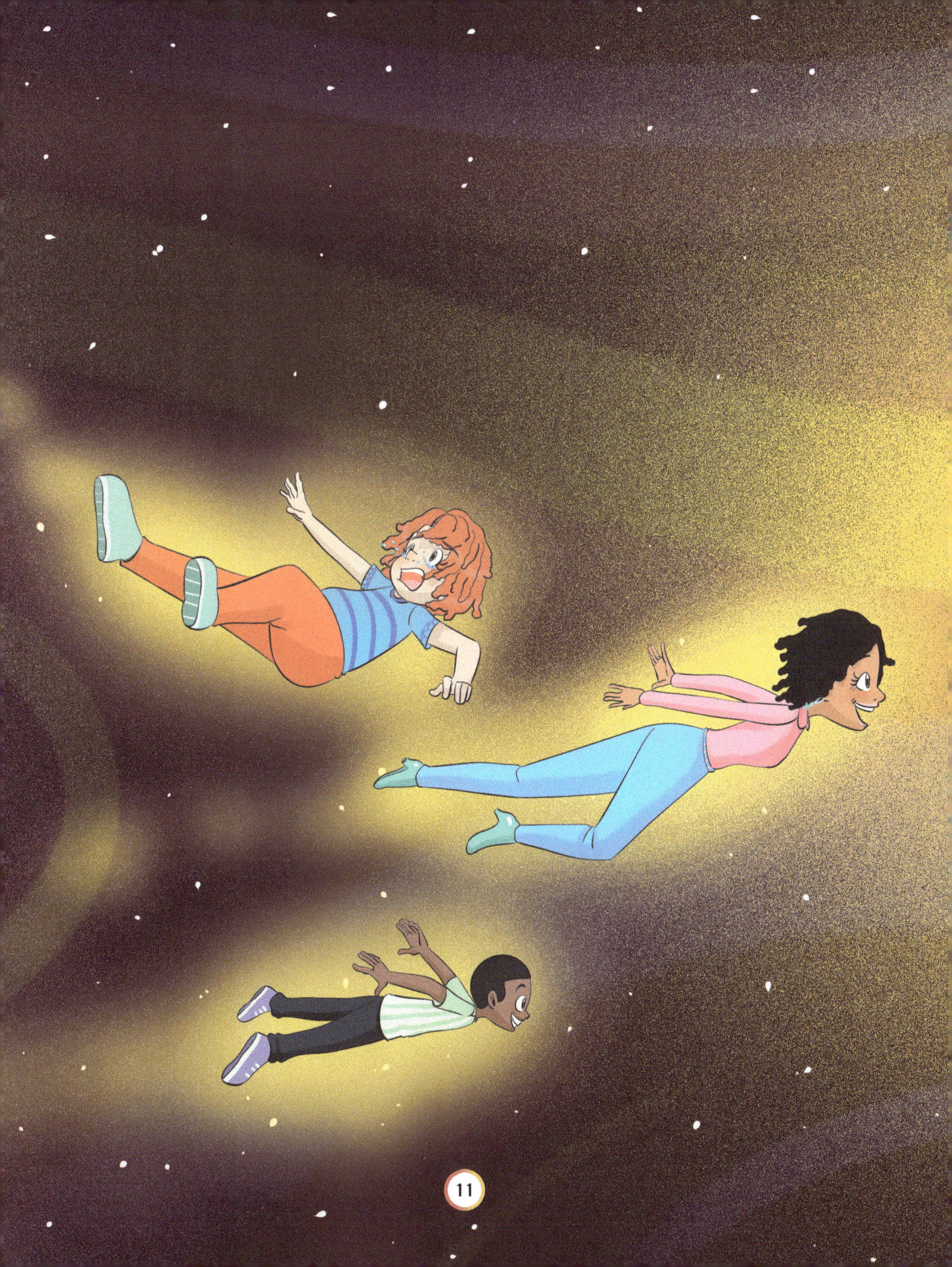

I LOVE

Jesus suffered to save us all.

14

He did this task because of the Fall.

16

He could've said "Nope! That's not My fault!"

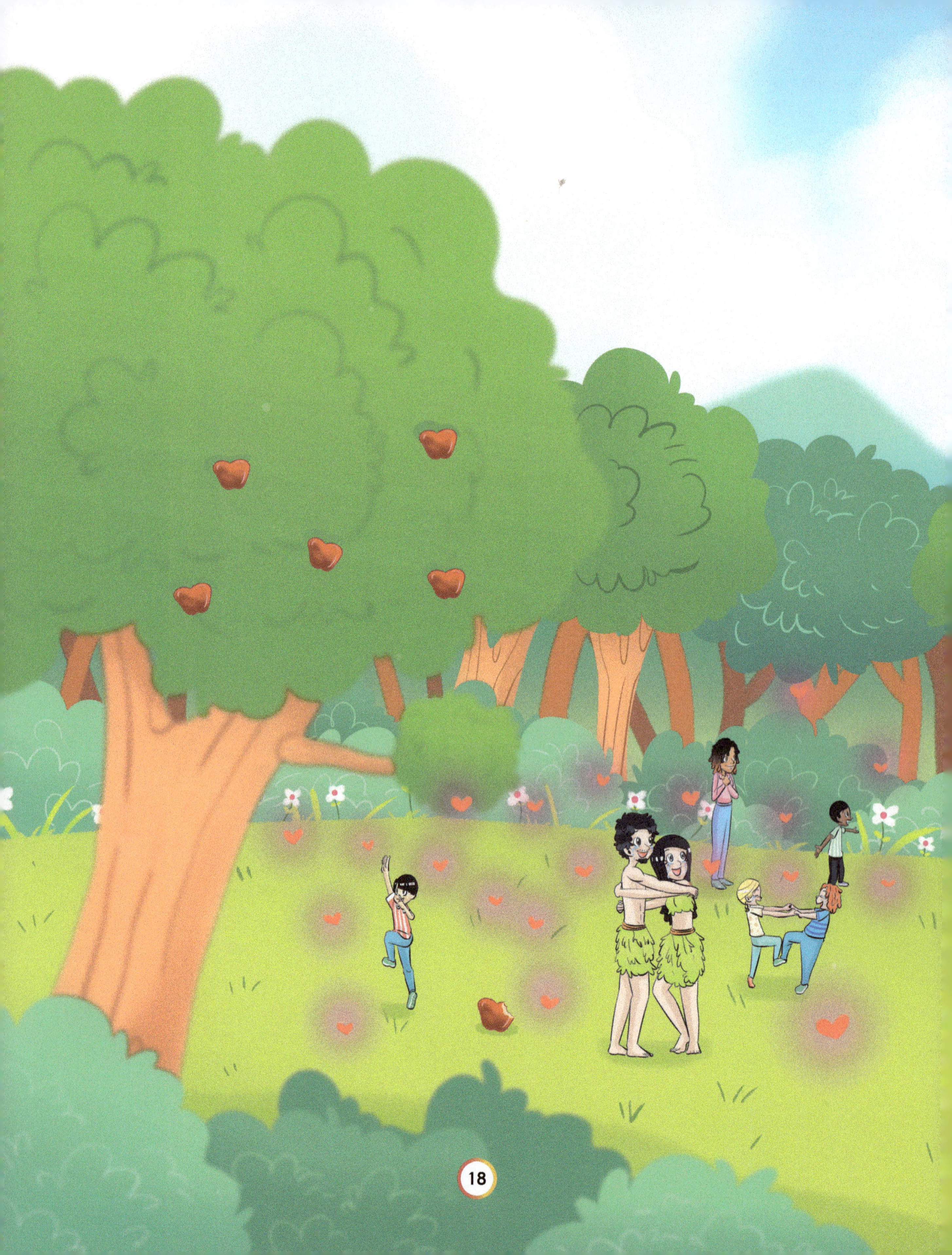

Instead, He chose GRACE to give us all.

**Tit for tat, Jesus is NOT about that.
Finding fault...**

Mrs. Jules

22

He just doesn't do that.

Like Peter, who lied, not once, but thrice.
He said he didn't know Him.
And he knew that wasn't right.

cockle-doo-a-doo!!!

Christ could've said,

"Nope! I don't know you!"

But instead, He said,

"Friend, you're still a part of My crew!"

**Tit for tat, Jesus is NOT about that.
Unforgiving…**

31

32

He's just not like that.

**Just like the Israelites,
who promised they wouldn't sin.**

35

We, too, have made promises, but we've broken them again and again.

37

He could've said,

"Yep! I'll break my vow!"

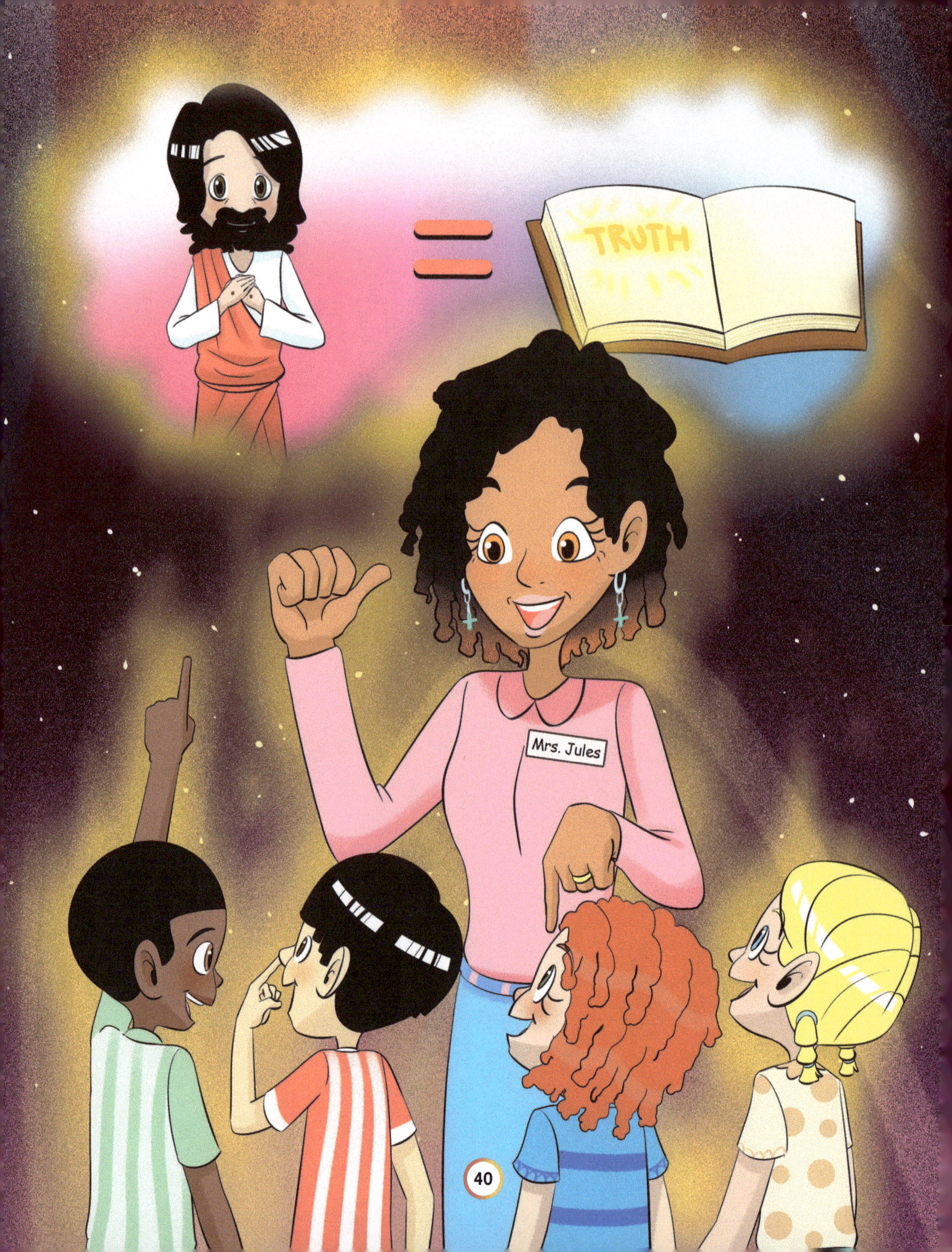
TRUTH
Mrs. Jules

**Only His name means *TRUTH*—
both yesterday and now.**

Tit for tat, Jesus is NOT about that.
Breaking His promises…

43

44

He just doesn't do that.

JESUS

His name means LOVE.

His name means KING.

Did you know He's esteemed you far above everything?

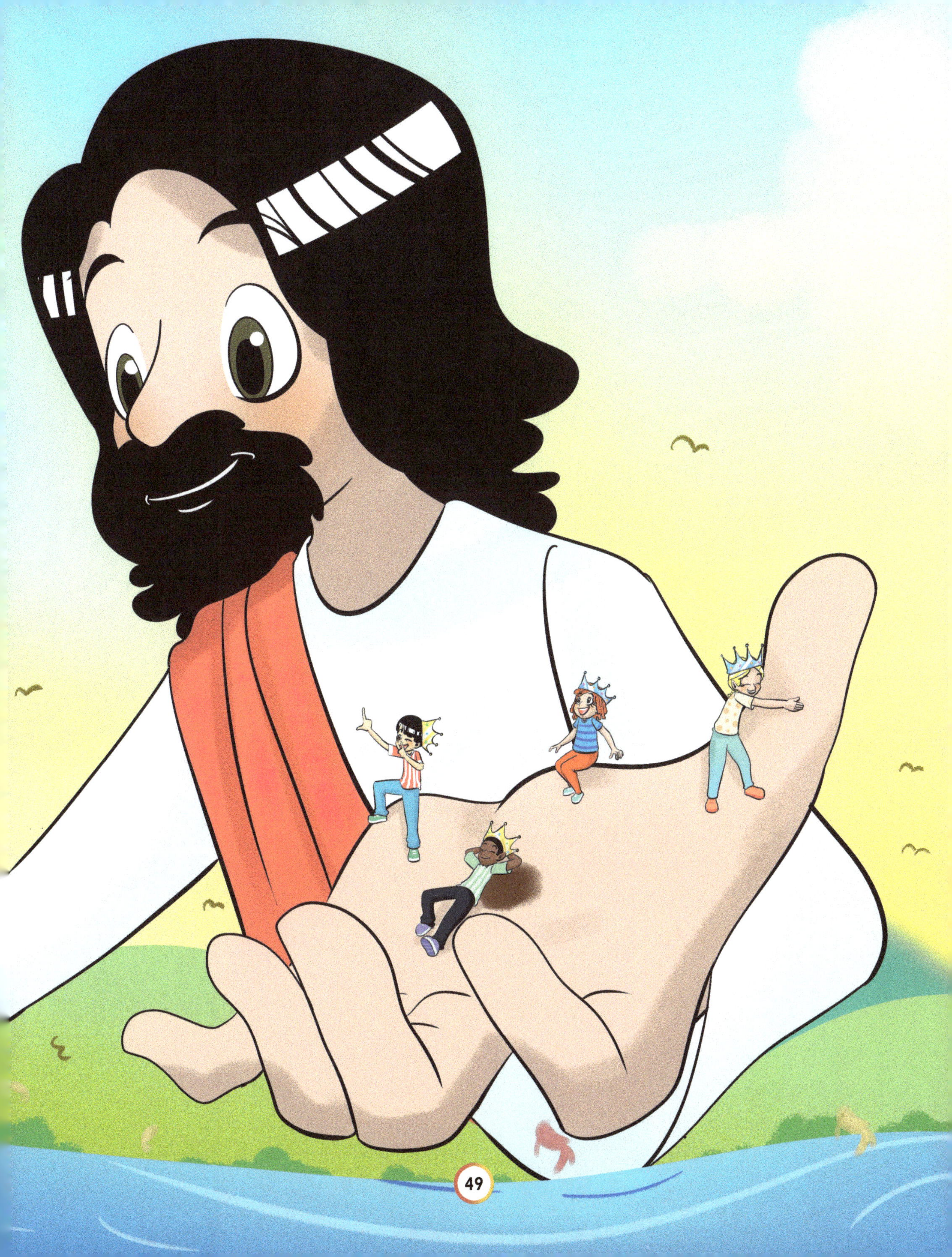

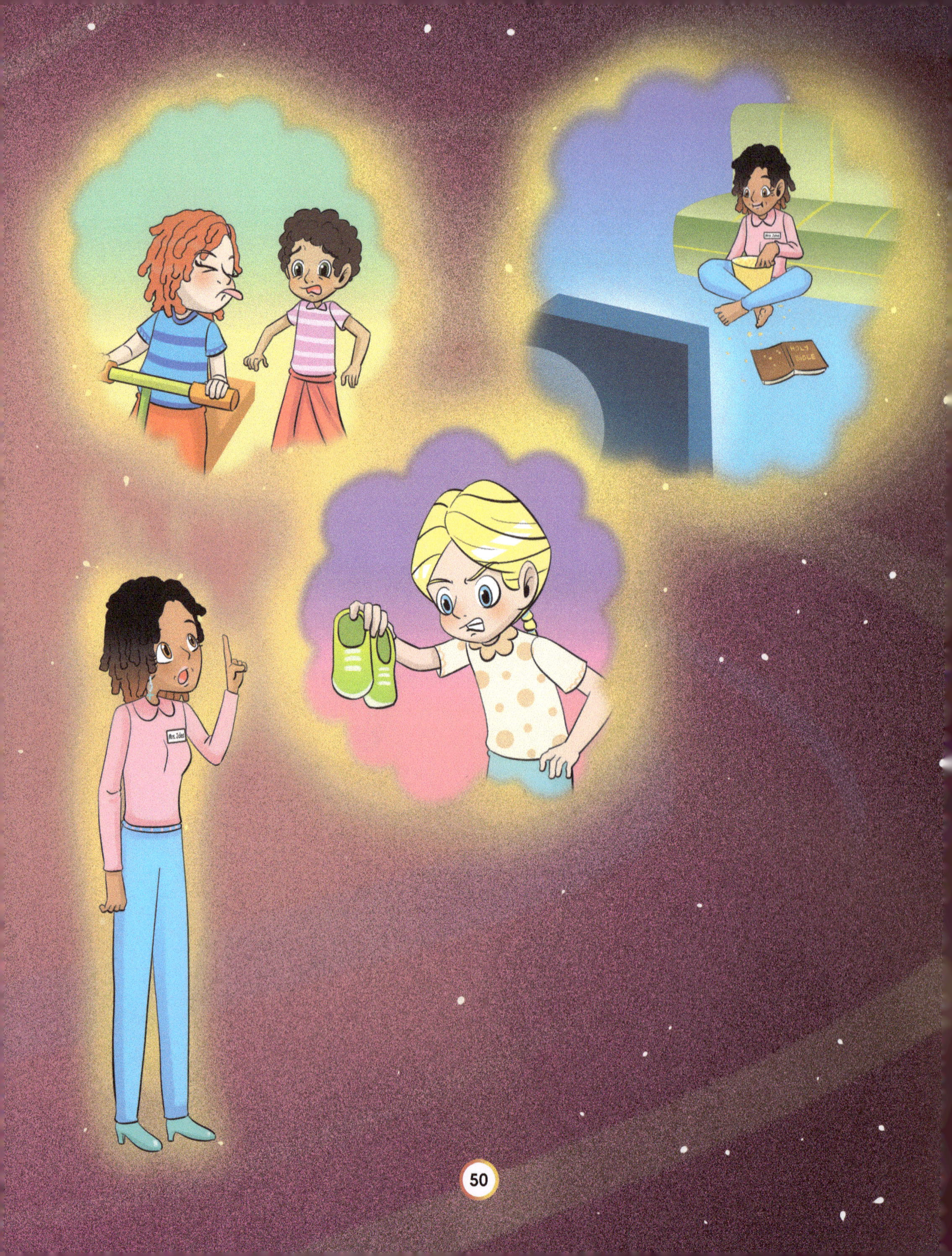
HOLY BIBLE

So whether you've done this ...

Or whether you've done that ...

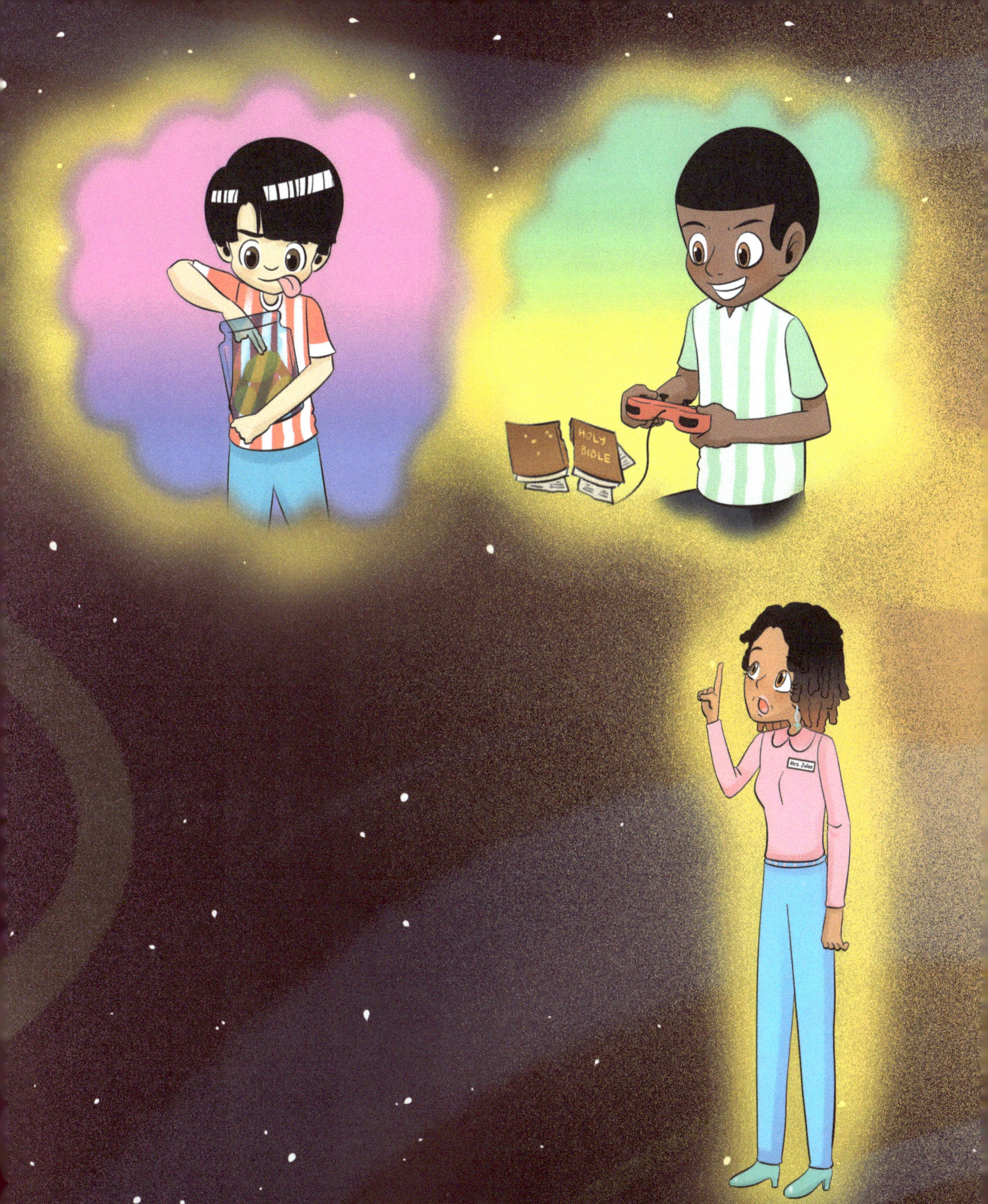
HOLY BIBLE
Mrs. Jules

Mrs. Jules

"I do to you what you've done to Me.
He will NEVER do that."

His actions show GRACE.

His words are forever TRUE.

58

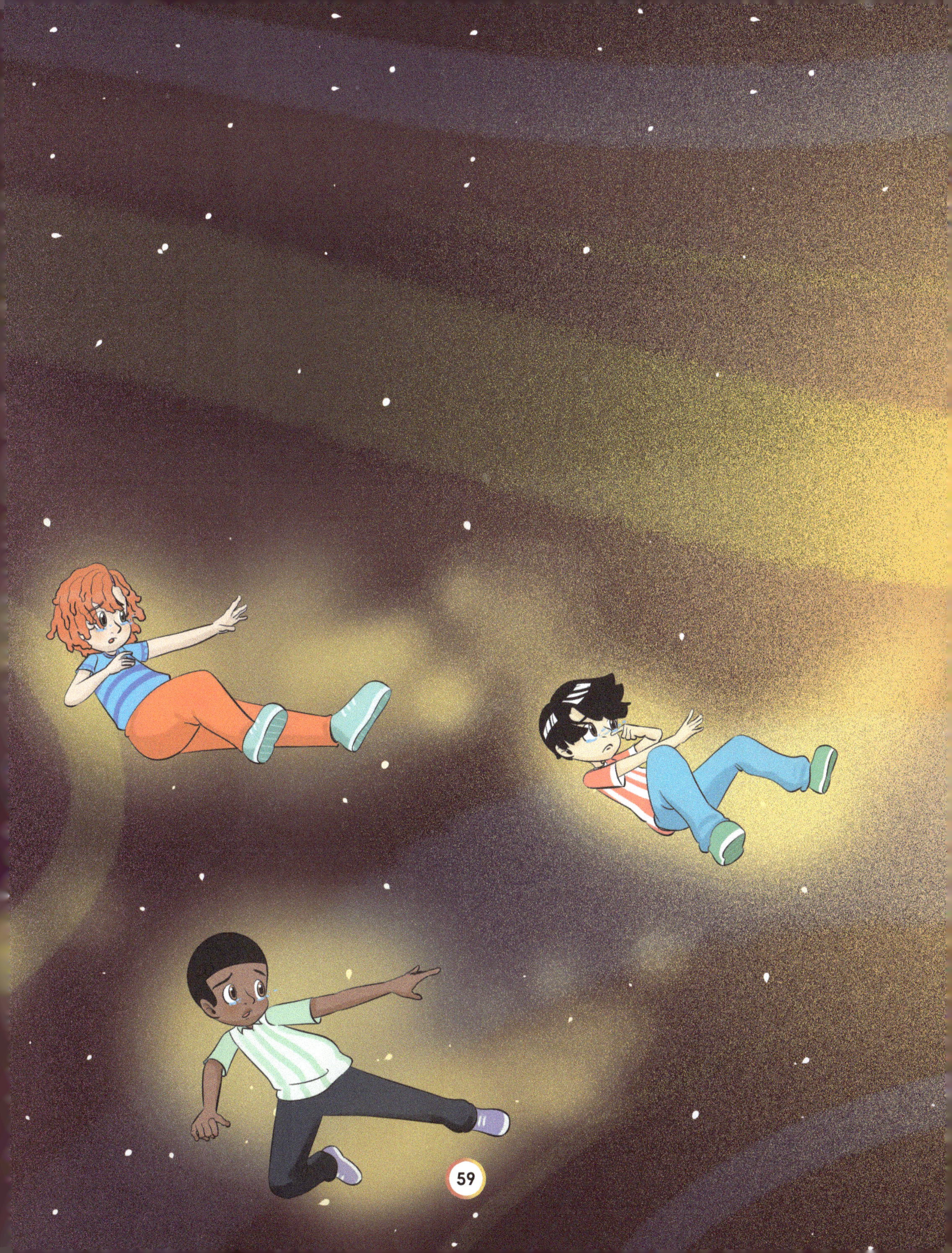

No matter how many your mistakes,

CLASS ROOM

61

62

He'll ALWAYS forgive you!

Out of his fullness we have all received grace in place of grace already given.
(John 1:16 NIV)

About the Author

Julia, a PK or pastor's kid and one out of nine siblings, wears several hats. With her stethoscope in one hand, Bible in the other, she incorporates her nursing, teaching, and writing passions in all her endeavors. For the past ten years, she has worked as a full-time nurse, holding a certification specialty in blood and bone marrow transplantation (BMTCN) and immunotherapy. Apart from her nursing responsibilities, she, alongside her husband, Mike, enjoys homeschooling their three children: Ariana, thirteen; PJ, eight; and Faith, five. She is also a test-item writer for a national certification nursing corporation, as well as a published author for Oncology Nursing Society (*Reflections on COVID-19 and Cancer Care: Stories by Oncology Nurses*).

Serving in the children's ministry at her local church is another hallmark fancy of hers. Additionally, along with her husband and eldest daughter, Ariana, she has taken part in serving internationally, coordinating both medical and youth discipleship mission projects with Future Generation International Missions Corporation (FGIM). She resides in Washington state with her husband and childhood sweetheart, whom she's been married to for fifteen years. Some of her hobbies include reading, journaling, dancing, traveling, and watching great movies (drama, action/adventure) and even K-dramas (Korean dramas). All who knows her can attest, whether it's caring for a sick patient in the hospital, homeschooling her three kiddos, or even leading a tug-of-war competition with a group of rambunctious youth, her life's intent is clear:

Trust in the Lord with all your heart; do not depend on your own understanding. Seek His will in all you do, and He will show you which paths to take. (Proverbs 3:5–6 NLT)

And she inspires others to do the same.
This is her first published children's book.

Printed in the USA
CPSIA information can be obtained
at www.ICGtesting.com
CBHW041018061224
18359CB00049B/793